KETO-DIET
COOKBOOK

For Beginners

Eat, Get Slimmer,
Look Younger, and
Adopt a Healthy Lifestyle

*Youth-Extending
Simple Recipes*

2 Week Meal Plan

*to Boost Energy
and Promote
Long-Term Wellness*

By Tara Broock (Tam' Brown)

03.12.24

Copyright Statement

Copyright © 2024 by Tara Broock. All rights reserved.

No part of this publication may be reproduced, distributed, or transmitted in any form or by any means, including photocopying, recording, or other electronic or mechanical methods, without the prior written permission of the publisher, except for brief quotations included in critical reviews and certain other non-commercial uses permitted by copyright law.

This book serves as a comprehensive guide to introduce beginners to the ketogenic diet. It features personally adapted recipes, meal plans, and practical suggestions that have been carefully compiled by the author.

Disclaimer

The information in this cookbook is intended for informational purposes only and should not be considered medical advice, diagnosis, or treatment. Readers are encouraged to consult their healthcare provider before beginning any dietary regimen, particularly if they have pre-existing health conditions.

The author and publisher are not liable for any misunderstanding or misuse of the information in this book or for any loss, injury, or damages caused by following the suggestions herein. The dietary and nutritional information provided in this book reflects the author's experiences and personal knowledge but should not replace professional advice. The Food and Drug Administration has not evaluated the statements and information provided.

The recipes are based on the author's personal interpretations and adaptations of ketogenic principles, and they are not guaranteed to be suitable for everyone. Nutritional information is provided for convenience and should not be used as a substitute for advice from professional nutritionists or healthcare providers.

TABLE OF CONTENTS

INTRODUCTION 6
    1. What is the keto diet? 6
    2. The science behind Keto and anti-aging 6
    3. Benefits of Keto for Beginners 6
    4. Personal Experience and Important Disclaimer 7

ANTI-AGIN BREAKFASTS 8
    Poached eggs, avocado, stewed sweet potato with chees 8
    Scrambled Eggs with Avocado Sauce, Potato pancakes, and Cheese 9
    Scrambled Eggs with Avocado Toast, Cherry Tomatoes, and Cheese 11
    Fluffy Omelette with Mushrooms, Tomatoes, and Cheese 12
    Delicious Egg Pancakes with Salmon 13
    Classic Oatmeal with Butter and Honey 14
    Fried Millet Porridge with Pumpkin and Honey 15
    Rejuvenating Buckwheat with Butter 16
    Youth-Enhancing Cheese Pancakes with Herbs 18
    Royal Spicy Cottage Cheese Spread 19
    Zucchini Pancakes with Nut Sauce 20
    Pumpkin Pancakes "Noble" 21
    Creamy Green Buckwheat Mousse with Banana and Berries 22
    Note: Important Information about Grains, Butter, and Sweets! 23

ANTI-AGIN LUNCHES 24
    Beetroot Salad "Empress" 24
    Classic Vinaigrette Salad 25
    Lentil Salad "Fantasy" with Avocado and Nuts 26
    Salad with Fried Eggplant (Aubergine) 27
    Note: How to Prepare Bone Broth for Quick Soup Making 28
    Youthful Collagen Soup for Thick Hair and Firm Skin 29
    Youthful Collagen Borscht with Chicken 30
    Youthful Fish Soup 31

Buckwheat with Mushrooms, Egg and Cheese 32

Spicy Vegetarian Rice with Vegetables 33

Potato Pizza with Cheese 34

Sea Bass Baked with Sweet Potatoes 35

Scrambled Eggs with Shrimp, Quinoa, and Avocado 36

Cauliflower Pizza with Cheese 37

Pasta with Cheese and Tomato Sauce 38

ANTI-AGIN DINNERS 39

Greek Salad with Shrimp 39

Nutritious Warm Zucchini Salad on a Green Bed 40

Lentil Salad "Fantasy" with Avocado and Nuts 41

Buckwheat with Liver Pancakes 42

Stewed Lentils with Onion and Carrots 43

Buckwheat with Mushrooms and Basil-Avocado Sauce 44

Stewed Liver with Vegetable Salad 45

Brown Rice with Shrimp and Salad 46

Scrambled Eggs with Shrimp and Vegetables 47

Spicy Stewed Lentils with Chicken 48

Hummus with Carrot and Cucumber Sticks 49

Baked Salmon with Salad 50

Fried Eggs with Shrimp, Quinoa, and Avocado 51

Chicken Liver Mousse with Quinoa and Carrots 52

ANTI-AGIN DESSERTS 53

Delicate Carrot Pie "Delight" 53

Homemade Chocolate 54

Pumpkin Chocolate Mousse 55

Carrot Cookies 56

Baked Apples with Honey and Nuts 57

Chocolate Banana Ice Cream 58

Stewed Pumpkin with Dried Apricots and Walnuts 59

Chocolate Pancakes 60

Chia Seed Pudding with Berries and Banana 61

Buckwheat Pancakes with Honey and Butter 62

Nutty "Hedgehogs" 63
Sourdough Bread with Butter and Herbal Tea 64
Flaxseed Buns 65
Fruit Salad with Coconut-Nut Dressing 67
Banana-Chocolate Cake 68

TIPS FOR SUCCESS ON THE KETO-DIET 69
How to Drink Water Correctly to Activate Natural Body Rejuvenation 69
Guide to Dairy Products 70
Food Combinations 71
    Food Combinations to Avoid 71
    Conditional Combinations: Suitable if You Do not Have Serious Health Issues 72
    Proper Food Combinations 73
10 Fake "Health Foods" Marketed as Healthy 74

CONCLUSION 77
ABOUT THE AUTHOR 78
YOUR REVIEW MEANS THE WORLD TO US 79

INTRODUCTION

1. **What is the keto diet?**
   - **Description of the keto diet**: The ketogenic (or keto diet) is a low-carbohydrate, high-fat diet designed to shift the body's primary energy source from carbohydrates to fat. The diet's core involves drastically reducing carbohydrate intake and increasing fat consumption, which leads to a metabolic state called ketosis.
   - **Main principles**: Normally, the body uses glucose (from carbohydrates) for energy. When carbohydrate intake is limited, the body starts breaking down fats into ketones, becoming the primary energy source.
   - **Purpose of the diet**: The main goals are weight loss, increased energy levels, improved cognitive function, and overall health maintenance.

2. **The science behind Keto and anti-aging**
   - **Ketosis and cellular metabolism**: During ketosis, the body uses ketone bodies, which are metabolized more efficiently than glucose. This reduces the formation of free radicals and oxidative stress, potentially slowing the aging process at the cellular level.
   - **Autophagy**: Studies suggest that ketosis promotes autophagy — a cellular "cleaning" process that removes damaged cellular components, which are then replaced with new ones. This is an important mechanism for combating premature aging.
   - **Brain and cognitive health**: Ketone bodies protect neurons and may reduce the risk of age-related neurodegenerative diseases like Alzheimer's.
   - **Cell regeneration and reduced inflammation**: The keto diet can help reduce chronic inflammation, which is a key factor in longevity and maintaining healthy, youthful skin.

3. **Benefits of Keto for Beginners**
   - **Rapid weight loss**: Beginners often experience quick weight loss on the keto diet due to the depletion of carbohydrate stores and the reduction of excess water retention.
   - **Increased energy levels**: Shifting to fat as the primary energy source helps maintain stable blood sugar levels, preventing energy crashes and fatigue.
   - **Reduced appetite**: The high fat and protein content of the keto diet helps promote satiety, making it easier to control portions and avoid overeating.

- **Improved focus and cognitive function**: With stabilized blood sugar and the use of ketones, many people experience enhanced mental clarity and concentration.
- **Better skin**: The keto diet's anti-inflammatory effects and promotion of cellular regeneration can improve skin health.
- **Decreased cravings for sweets**: One of the major benefits for beginners is the reduction in sugar cravings. As the body adjusts to burning fat for fuel, the need for constant glucose, and therefore sugary snacks, diminishes significantly.

4. Personal Experience and Important Disclaimer

All the recipes in this book have been thoughtfully adapted by me, Tara Broock, based on my personal experience and preferences. For the past 20-25 years, I have followed these dietary principles and used these recipes in my daily life. Thanks to this lifestyle, I have been able to maintain excellent health, keep my weight stable, and, as many say, appear younger than my age. These recipes have not only supported my overall well-being but have also allowed me to enjoy delicious, nourishing meals every day.

However, it is important to note that each person's body is unique, and what works well for me might not suit everyone. If you have any chronic health conditions or specific dietary needs, I strongly recommend consulting with your doctor or a qualified dietician before making any significant changes to your diet. The author is not responsible for any outcomes resulting from the use of the recipes and suggestions provided in this book.

ANTI-AGIN BREAKFASTS

Poached eggs, avocado, stewed sweet potato with chees
(1 portion, 20 minutes, gluten-free)

Ingredients:
- 2 eggs
- 1 ripe soft avocado
- 1 oz. (30 g) of fatty cheese
- 1 sweet potato
- 1 tsp butter (ghee)

Instructions:
1. Peel the sweet potato and cut it into thin slices. Simmer with oil and a few drops of water under a closed lid.
   Sweet potato goes well with paprika and coriander spices.
2. Carefully crack the eggs into a cup.
3. Pour water into the frying pan (about half) and when the water boils, pour 2 eggs in. Turn off the water and let the whites set for about 2-3 minutes.
4. Combine eggs, Sweet potato, cheese and avocado

Nutritional Information (per serving):
Calories: 435 kcal, Fats: 35g, Carbs: 24g, Protein: 17g, Fiber: 9g, Cholesterol: 370mg, Sodium: 190mg, Potassium: 900mg

Scrambled Eggs with Avocado Sauce, Potato pancakes, and Cheese

(1 serving, 40 minutes, gluten-free)

Ingredients:
- 2 large eggs
- 1 ripe avocado
- 2 garlic cloves (optional)
- ½ bunch of cilantro (for the sauce)
- Juice of ⅓ lemon
- Fresh cilantro (or any greens you prefer, such as spinach, kale, etc.)
- Salt to taste
- Ghee (clarified butter)
- Tomatoes (cherry tomatoes)
- Sheep's cheese

Recipe for Potato pancakes on the next page

Instructions:
1. Grease the skillet with ghee and pour in the eggs. Stir them immediately and cook for 1-2 minutes, then turn off the heat.
2. Blend the avocado into a smooth paste. Add garlic, cilantro, salt, and lemon juice to the avocado and blend again.
3. Combine the scrambled eggs, potato pancakes, avocado sauce, tomatoes, greens, and cheese on a plate.

Nutritional Information (per serving):
Calories: 450 kcal, Fats: 35g, Carbs: 12g, Protein: 18g, Fiber: 7g, Cholesterol: 380mg, Sodium: 390mg, Potassium: 900mg

Potato Pancakes
(2 servings, 30 minutes, gluten-free)

Ingredients:
- 2 large potatoes
- 1 large egg
- Salt, black pepper to taste
- 2-3 tbsp gluten-free flour (e.g., rice flour, chestnut flour)
- 1 tsp ghee (clarified butter)

Instructions:
1. Grate the potatoes on a coarse grater and squeeze the excess liquid.
2. Form small pancakes on a baking sheet greased with ghee.
3. Bake in the oven for 25-30 minutes at 350°F (180°C). Try to avoid over-browning.

Nutritional Information (per serving):
Calories: 210 kcal, Fats: 7g, Carbs: 34g, Protein: 5g, Fiber: 4g, Cholesterol: 55mg, Sodium: 210mg, Potassium: 620mg.

Scrambled Eggs with Avocado Toast, Cherry Tomatoes, and Cheese
(1 serving, 10 minutes)

Ingredients:
- 2 large eggs
- 1 ripe avocado
- 2 garlic cloves (optional)
- ½ bunch of cilantro (for the sauce)
- Juice of ⅓ lemon
- Fresh cilantro (or any greens you prefer, such as spinach, kale, or arugula)
- Salt to taste
- Ghee (clarified butter)
- Cherry tomatoes
- 1 slice of whole-grain bread

Instructions:
1. Grease the skillet with ghee and pour in the eggs. Stir immediately, cook for 1-2 minutes, and then turn off the heat.
2. Blend the avocado into a smooth paste.
3. Add garlic, cilantro, salt, and lemon juice to the avocado and blend again.
4. Combine the scrambled eggs, avocado toast, cherry tomatoes, and cheese on a plate.

Nutritional Information (per serving):
Calories: 380 kcal, Fats: 28g, Carbs: 18g, Protein: 14g, Fiber: 8g, Cholesterol: 390mg, Sodium: 250mg, Potassium: 930mg.

Fluffy Omelette with Mushrooms, Tomatoes, and Cheese
(1 serving, 15 minutes, gluten-free)

Ingredients:
- 2 large eggs
- 3-4 mushrooms (e.g., button mushrooms or any other)
- 4-6 cherry tomatoes (or 1 medium tomato)
- 1 oz (30 g) grated soft cheese
- 1 ripe avocado
- 2 garlic cloves (optional)
- ½ bunch of cilantro
- Salt to taste
- Juice of ⅓ lemon

Instructions:

1. Omelette:
Blend the 2 eggs in a blender until fluffy.
Grease a frying pan with oil, fry the mushrooms, and then add the tomatoes.
Pour the eggs into the frying pan and let them set slightly.
Add the grated cheese to one-half of the omelette, cook for another 2 minutes, and then fold the omelette in half.

2. Avocado Sauce:
Blend the avocado into a smooth paste.
Add garlic, cilantro, salt, and lemon juice to the avocado and blend again.

3. Spread the avocado sauce on a slice of whole grain bread drizzled with olive oil and serve alongside the omelette.

Nutritional Information (per serving):
Calories: 410 kcal, Fats: 33g, Carbs: 12g, Protein: 16g, Fiber: 7g, Cholesterol: 390mg, Sodium: 330mg, Potassium: 960mg.

Delicious Egg Pancakes with Salmon
(2-3 servings, 15 minutes, gluten-free)

Ingredients:
- 7 oz (200 g) lightly salted salmon
- 5 large eggs
- Salt to taste
- 1.8 oz (50 g) spinach (or any leafy greens of your choice, such as arugula, kale, etc.)
- 1 tbsp ghee (clarified butter)

Instructions:
1. Beat the eggs in a blender, adding a pinch of salt.
2. Grease the frying pan with ghee, and pour in a little egg mixture to create a thin pancake, about 0.2 inch (0.5 cm) thick.
3. Cook for about 3 minutes, until the pancake sets. Once the pancake is cooked, place the salmon and greens on top. Roll the pancake into a tube, transfer it to a plate, and cut it in half.

Nutritional Information (per serving):
Calories: 320 kcal, Fats: 25g, Carbs: 2g, Protein: 23g, Fiber: 1g, Cholesterol: 0,42g, Sodium: 0,58g, Potassium: 0,6g.

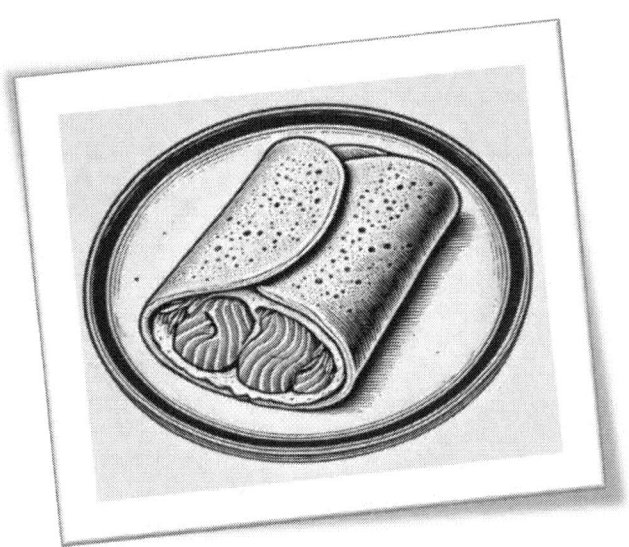

Classic Oatmeal with Butter and Honey
(2 servings, 20 minutes, vegetarian)

Ingredients:
- 7 oz (200 g) long-cooking oatmeal (20 minutes)
- 7 oz (200 g) of any plant-based milk (optional)
- Water
- Salt
- 1-1.5 tbsp (15-20 g) butter
- 1 tsp ghee (clarified butter) for cooking
- 1 tsp honey

Instructions:
1. Pour boiling water over the oatmeal, covering it, and let it sit for about an hour with a lid. You can also soak the oatmeal overnight.
2. Heat the milk and add the soaked oatmeal. Cook for 4-5 minutes until done, and then serve in a bowl with butter and honey.

Nutritional Information (per serving):
Calories: 260 kcal, Fats: 10g, Carbs: 38g, Protein: 5g, Fiber: 4g, Cholesterol: 20mg, Sodium: 100mg, Potassium: 180mg.

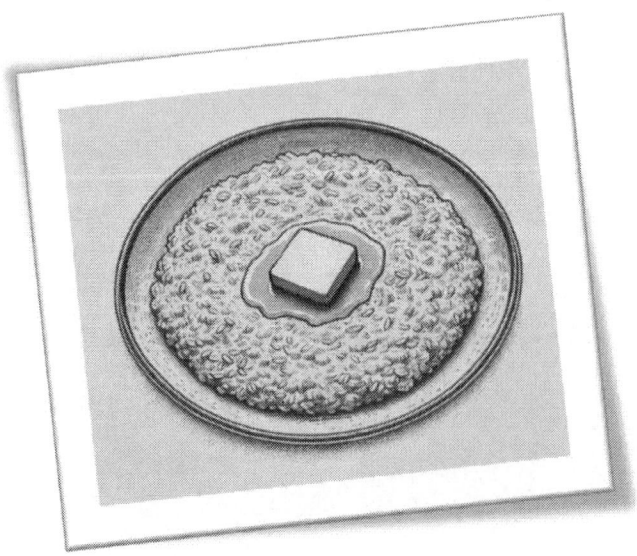

Fried Millet Porridge with Pumpkin and Honey
(2 servings, 20 minutes, gluten-free, vegetarian)

Ingredients:
- Water
- 7 oz (200 g) millet
- 10.5 oz (300 g) pumpkin
- 1-1.5 tbsp (15-20 g) butter
- Salt to taste
- 1 tsp honey
- 2 tsp butter for frying
- Spices to taste (turmeric, paprika, saffron)

Instructions:
1. Cover the millet with water, ensuring the water level is 1-1.5 inches (3-4 cm) above the millet. Bring to a boil, and then drain the water to remove the bitterness. Add clean water, bring to a boil again, and turn off the heat, covering the pot with a lid.
2. Peel and dice the pumpkin into small cubes. Grease a pan with butter, add the pumpkin pieces and a pinch of salt, and then cover with a lid. Simmer for about 5 minutes, stirring occasionally.
3. In a separate pan, greased with butter, place the millet and add a little water. Cover and cook until done. Then, transfer to a plate, season with salt, top with butter, and add the stewed pumpkin along with honey on top.

Nutritional Information (per serving):
Calories: 521 kcal, Fats: 15.75g, Carbs: 86.5g, Protein: 11g, Fiber: 6g, Cholesterol: 0.03g, Sodium: 0.02g, Potassium: 0.42g.

Rejuvenating Buckwheat with Butter
(2 servings, 10 minutes, gluten-free, vegetarian)

Ingredients:
- 7 oz (200 g) buckwheat
- Water
- Salt to taste
- 1-1.5 tbsp (15-20 g) butter
- 1 tsp ghee (clarified butter) for cooking
- 1 tsp honey

Instructions:
1. Pour boiling water over the buckwheat, cover with a lid, and let it sit for about an hour. Afterward, grease a pan with butter, add the buckwheat, and heat it while stirring.
2. Transfer the buckwheat to a plate, add the butter and honey on top.

Nutritional Information (per serving):
Calories: 355 kcal, Fats: 14g, Carbs: 48g, Protein: 11g, Fiber: 6g, Cholesterol: 0.04g, Sodium: 0.02g, Potassium: 0.33g.

Glowing Skin Flaxseed Porridge
(2 servings, 10 minutes, gluten-free, vegetarian)

Ingredients:
- 8 tbsp ground flaxseeds
- 1 ⅔ cups (400 ml) plant-based milk (almond, oat, coconut, etc.)
- A pinch of salt
- 1 banana
- 1 tsp honey
- 1 tbsp ghee (clarified butter)

Instructions:
1. Blend the flaxseeds in a blender. Bring the plant-based milk to a boil, and then slowly add the flaxseeds while stirring. Remove from heat and let the flaxseeds absorb the liquid for about 2 minutes.
2. If the porridge is too thick, add a bit more hot milk. Serve the porridge on a plate, season with salt, and top with sliced banana and ghee.

Nutritional Information (per serving):
Calories: 369 kcal, Fats: 27.5g, Carbs: 27.6g, Protein: 9.5g, Fiber: 9.5g, Cholesterol: 0g, Sodium: 0.002g, Potassium: 0.335g.

Youth-Enhancing Cheese Pancakes with Herbs
(2 servings, 15 minutes, gluten-free)

Ingredients:
- 24.5 oz (700 g) cottage cheese
- 1-1.8 oz (30-50 g) any gluten-free flour (rice, etc.)
- 5 sprigs of fresh dill
- A pinch of salt
- 1 egg
- 1 tbsp ghee (clarified butter)

Instructions:
1. Mix all ingredients together until smooth and creamy. Chop the dill finely and stir it into the batter.
2. Grease a frying pan with ghee and cook the cheese pancakes for about 4 minutes on one side. Flip and cook on the other side until golden.

Nutritional Information (per serving):
Calories: 430 kcal, Fats: 24g, Carbs: 25g, Protein: 30g, Fiber: 2g, Cholesterol: 0.15g, Sodium: 0.04g, Potassium: 0.15g.

Royal Spicy Cottage Cheese Spread
(2 servings, 10 minutes, gluten-free)

Ingredients:
- 14 oz (400 g) full-fat cottage cheese
- 1 cucumber
- ½ bunch of fresh dill
- Salt to taste
- 2 garlic cloves (optional)

Instructions:
1. Finely chop the cucumber and dill.
2. Mince the garlic. Add all the ingredients to the cottage cheese and mix thoroughly.
3. The spicy spread is ready! It is best enjoyed as a standalone dish or as a dip.

Nutritional Information (per serving):
Calories: 215 kcal, Fats: 12g, Carbs: 8g, Protein: 18g, Fiber: 1g, Cholesterol: 0.04g, Sodium: 0.03g, Potassium: 0.2g.

Zucchini Pancakes with Nut Sauce

(2 servings, 30 minutes, gluten-free)

Ingredients:
- 1 medium zucchini
- 1 egg
- 3 tbsp any gluten-free flour (rice, etc.)
- Pepper to taste
- Salt to taste
- Paprika (optional)
- 2 oz hard cheese, grated
- 2 tsp ghee (clarified butter) for frying
- ¼ cup cashews (soaked overnight) and soaked in boiling water for 1 hour
- 3 tbsp water
- A few basil leaves (optional)

Instructions:
1. Grate the zucchini and squeeze out the excess liquid. Add the egg, flour, pepper, and salt, and mix well.
2. Grease a frying pan with ghee and spread the batter in portions to make small pancakes.
   Tip: I usually use two pans at once to speed up the process.
3. Cover with a lid and fry for 2-4 minutes on one side, then flip and fry until golden. Grate the cheese over the pancakes and sprinkle them on top.
4. For the sauce, blend the soaked cashews with a pinch of salt, water, and basil until smooth.

Nutritional Information (per serving):
Calories: 340 kcal, Fats: 25g, Carbs: 20g, Protein: 12g, Fiber: 4g, Cholesterol: 0.09g, Sodium: 0.04g, Potassium: 0.25g.

Pumpkin Pancakes "Noble"
(2 servings, 20 minutes, gluten-free)

Ingredients:
- 21 oz (600 g) pumpkin
- 1 tart-sweet apple
- 3 tbsp any gluten-free flour (rice, etc.)
- 1 egg
- Salt and pepper to taste
- 1 tbsp butter or ghee for frying

Instructions:
1. Grate the pumpkin on a coarse grater, then grate the apple and squeeze out the excess juice. Add the raw egg, flour, salt, and pepper to the mixture. Mix well.
2. Grease a frying pan with butter or ghee.
3. Spoon the batter into the pan, forming small pancakes.
4. Fry the pancakes on each side until golden, covering the pan with a lid. Be careful not to overcook them.
5. Serve the pancakes with butter and a fragrant herbal tea.

Nutritional Information (per serving):
Calories: 230 kcal, Fats: 8g, Carbs: 32g, Protein: 6g, Fiber: 5g, Cholesterol: 0.08g, Sodium: 0.03g, Potassium: 0.4g.

Creamy Green Buckwheat Mousse with Banana and Berries

(2 servings, 5 minutes, gluten-free, vegetarian)

Ingredients:
- 10.5 oz (300 g) sprouted green buckwheat
- A handful of any berries (blueberries, raspberries, blackberries)
- 2 bananas
- 10 tbsp coconut milk

Instructions:
1. Preparation (16-24 hours): Soak 8.8 oz (250 g) of green buckwheat overnight in cold water, then refrigerate. In the morning, rinse the buckwheat several times to remove any residue. Cover it with a cloth and let it sprout. Once short sprouts appear, the buckwheat is ready to use.
2. Blend the sprouted green buckwheat with the bananas and coconut milk until smooth. Serve the mousse in a bowl and garnish with the berries and banana slices.

Nutritional Information (per serving):
Calories: 370 kcal, Fats: 12g, Carbs: 62g, Protein: 7g, Fiber: 8g, Cholesterol: 0g, Sodium: 0.003g, Potassium: 0.45g

Note: Important Information about Grains, Butter, and Sweets!

If you have not been consuming butter regularly until now, start with 10-15 grams and monitor your sensations. You will soon understand how well your body absorbs butter.

***After consuming butter with your porridge, watch for the following signs**:
- Nausea
- Stomach heaviness
- Loss of appetite

If you notice any of these symptoms, reduce the amount of butter you consume. Butter should be eaten no more than 30 grams, 3-4 times per week.

To ensure that the butter is properly absorbed and benefits your body — for example, as a building block for hormones and the linings of internal organs — your body needs oxygen. The simplest way to ensure this is through a walk in fresh air for at least 30-40 minutes. The walk should be continuous without stops.

Sugar (honey) and grains are incompatible, as this combination stimulates an acidic environment that promotes the growth of harmful bacteria. To help restore gut flora, it is recommended to limit honey to 1 teaspoon.

*However, if you have serious inflammatory processes in the body or chronic diseases, try to **avoid adding honey, sugar, or fruits** to your porridge.

*Dairy products, including fermented ones, also do not pair well with grains. Therefore, it is best to use any plant-based milk when preparing porridge.

ANTI-AGIN LUNCHES

Beetroot Salad "Empress"
(2 servings, 10 minutes, gluten-free)

Ingredients:
- 1 boiled beetroot
- 1 tart-sweet apple
- A handful of any nuts (cashews, pine nuts, walnuts)
- 1 oz (30 g) of any rich cheese (Parmesan, sheep's cheese, goat cheese, mozzarella)
- A handful of fresh greens (cilantro, arugula, kale, romaine, etc.)
- Juice of ⅓ lemon
- Olive oil for dressing
- Salt to taste

Instructions:
1. Soak the nuts in water before preparing the salad.
2. **Tip**: Walnuts are best soaked overnight, cashews can be soaked for an hour, and pine nuts do not require soaking. In a pinch, you can pour boiling water over the nuts for 5-10 minutes before using them.
3. Peel the apple and beetroot, and then slice them into small pieces. Finely chop the greens. Add the cheese and nuts. Serve the salad dressed with olive oil and lemon juice, and season with salt to taste.

Nutritional Information (per serving):
Calories: 290 kcal, Fats: 18g, Carbs: 25g, Protein: 8g, Fiber: 6g, Cholesterol: 0.01g, Sodium: 0.02g, Potassium: 0.5g.

Classic Vinaigrette Salad
(2-3 servings, 30 minutes, gluten-free, vegetarian)

Ingredients:
- 3 medium boiled potatoes
- 2 medium boiled carrots
- 1 large boiled beet
- 4-5 pickles (or 6-8 tbsp sauerkraut)
- 1 onion
- 1 green tart-sweet apple
- Salt to taste
- 5 tbsp sunflower oil

Instructions:
1. Peel the boiled vegetables and apple, and dice all the ingredients. Add the diced pickles or sauerkraut.
2. Serve the salad, dressed with sunflower oil, and season with salt to taste.

Nutritional Information (per serving):
Calories: 250 kcal, Fats: 14g, Carbs: 28g, Protein: 4g, Fiber: 5g, Cholesterol: 0g, Sodium: 0.4g, Potassium: 0.8g.

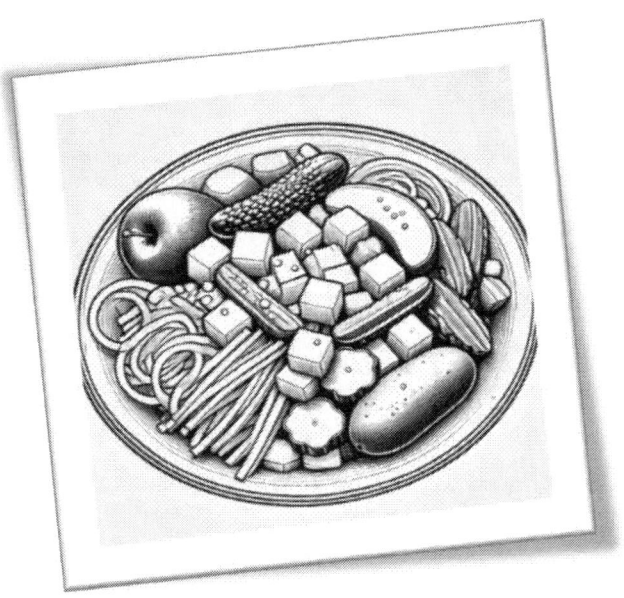

Lentil Salad "Fantasy" with Avocado and Nuts
(2 servings, 10 minutes, gluten-free, vegetarian)

Ingredients:
- 3.5 oz (100 g) sprouted lentils (mung beans)
- 1 ripe avocado (can substitute with cucumber)
- 1 tart-sweet apple, peeled
- 0.7 oz (20 g) any nuts (cashews, pine nuts, walnuts)
- A handful of fresh greens (cilantro, arugula, kale, romaine, etc.)
- Juice of ¼ lemon (optional)
- 2 tbsp olive oil or pumpkin oil for dressing
- Salt to taste

Instructions:
1. Soak the nuts in water before preparing the salad.
2. **Tip**: Walnuts are best-soaked overnight, cashews for an hour, and pine nuts do not require soaking. If you are in a hurry, pour boiling water over the nuts for 5-10 minutes before using them.
3. Mash the avocado with a fork, cut the apple into small cubes, and finely chop the greens. Mix all ingredients together with the sprouted lentils and nuts. Before serving, dress the salad with oil and lemon juice, and season with salt.

Nutritional Information (per serving):
Calories: 330 kcal, Fats: 23g, Carbs: 23g, Protein: 9g, Fiber: 8g, Cholesterol: 0g, Sodium: 0.02g, Potassium: 0.5g.

Salad with Fried Eggplant (Aubergine)
(3-4 servings, 15-20 minutes, gluten-free)

Ingredients:
- 1 eggplant (aubergine)
- 2 boiled eggs
- 1 raw carrot
- ½ onion (optional)
- 2 garlic cloves (optional)
- 3 ripe tomatoes
- 3 cucumbers
- A handful of any fresh greens or a mix of different herbs you like (dill, parsley, cilantro, etc.)
- 4 tbsp fragrant cold-pressed sunflower oil
- 1 tsp ghee (clarified butter)

Instructions:
1. Slice the eggplant (aubergine) into wedges, add 1 tsp of oil to the pan, and fry over medium heat until golden on both sides. Then season with salt and cut the wedges into smaller pieces.
2. Grate the carrot and chop the greens. Slice the cucumbers and tomatoes. Then slice the onion into rings and press the garlic through a garlic press (if using).
3. Chop the eggs and mix all the ingredients.
4. Dress your delightful salad with the fragrant sunflower oil and add sea salt.

Nutritional Information (per serving):
Calories: 210 kcal, Fats: 15g, Carbs: 14g, Protein: 6g, Fiber: 5g, Cholesterol: 0.12g, Sodium: 0.03g, Potassium: 0.5g.

Note: How to Prepare Bone Broth for Quick Soup Making

Once a month, I prepare collagen-rich bone broths for healthy hair and nails. I dedicate about 8-12 hours to making it. During that time, the collagen fully transfers into the broth, allowing maximum absorption.

I usually make about 4-5 liters at once and freeze them for later use.

*Here is another secret to turning your bone broth into a true youth elixir: **Apple cider vinegar** added during cooking. I will explain the proportions below.

These soups will always save you during stressful situations, such as hair loss and post-flu recovery.

Thanks to this preparation, cooking any soup takes only 15 minutes.

For bone broth preparation, take about 4.4 lbs (2 kg) of chicken feet or bones and place them in cold water. This can be any poultry or animal (turkey, lamb, veal, and beef). *It is best to use organic, hormone-free bones and joints. However, if you do not have access to organic products boil the bones or feet for about 20 minutes and then drain the water, replacing it with fresh water.*

Next, bring it to a boil again and add 2-3 tbsp of apple cider vinegar per 3-4 liters of water. Cover with a lid, reduce the heat, and simmer for 8-12 hours.

Strain the broth and freeze it in portions of about 1 liter each.

This same system can be applied to fish bone broth (for fish soups).

If you love fish soup, try making bone broth using fish skins, spines, and heads.

Youthful Collagen Soup for Thick Hair and Firm Skin
(4 servings, 30 minutes, gluten-free)

Ingredients:
- 1.5 liters of pre-prepared bone broth
- 3.5 oz (100 g) cooked rice
- 2 garlic cloves
- 3.5 oz (100 g) shrimp or chicken
- 1 onion
- 1 carrot
- 2 boiled eggs
- 1 tsp ghee (clarified butter)
- A handful of sturdy leafy greens (kale, spinach, etc.)
- Salt and spices to taste

Instructions:
1. Finely chop the onion, grate the carrot, and mince the garlic. Sauté the vegetables in ghee, adding a small amount of water.
2. Bring the bone broth to a boil. Add the cooked rice and shrimp or chicken. After 10 minutes, add the sautéed vegetables, chopped boiled eggs, and greens. Season with salt and spices to taste.

Nutritional Information (per serving):
Calories: 220 kcal, Fats: 10g, Carbs: 16g, Protein: 14g, Fiber: 2g, Cholesterol: 0.25g, Sodium: 0.04g, Potassium: 0.4g.

Youthful Collagen Borscht with Chicken
(2-4 servings, 30 minutes, gluten-free)

Ingredients:
- 2 liters of pre-prepared bone broth
- 7 oz (200 g) chicken breast
- 1 medium cabbage
- 1 tomato
- 1 beetroot
- 1 carrot
- 1 onion
- 3 garlic cloves
- Coriander, cumin, paprika, bay leaf
- 1 tbsp ghee (clarified butter)
- 4 tbsp soaked lentils or mung beans (soaked overnight)

Instructions:
1. Boil the shredded cabbage until half-cooked.
2. Sauté the diced vegetables with spices in ghee, then add them to the cabbage.
3. Cut the chicken into pieces and add it to the soup.
4. Add the soaked lentils or mung beans, cook the borscht until all ingredients are fully cooked, and finally, add a bay leaf for flavor.

Nutritional Information (per serving):
Calories: 240 kcal, Fats: 12g, Carbs: 15g, Protein: 18g, Fiber: 6g, Cholesterol: 0.12g, Sodium: 0.05g, Potassium: 0.6g.

Youthful Fish Soup
(4 servings, 20 minutes, gluten-free)

Ingredients:
- 1.5 liters of pre-prepared fish bone broth (made from fish skins, fins, and heads)
- 2-3 pieces of any fish (halibut, salmon, cod, etc.)
- 1 onion
- 2 boiled eggs
- 1.8 oz (50 g) cooked rice
- 1 tsp ghee (clarified butter)
- A handful of sturdy leafy greens (kale, spinach, etc.)
- Bay leaf (optional)

Instructions:
1. Bring the bone broth to a boil, add the fish and finely chopped onion.
2. After 10 minutes, add the cooked rice and chopped greens. Cut the boiled eggs in half.
3. Check that the fish, onion, and greens are fully cooked.
4. Serve the soup with boiled eggs.

Nutritional Information (per serving):
Calories: 180 kcal, Fats: 8g, Carbs: 14g, Protein: 16g, Fiber: 2g, Cholesterol: 0.18g, Sodium: 0.04g, Potassium: 0.4g.

Buckwheat with Mushrooms, Egg and Cheese
(2 servings, 20 minutes, gluten-free)

Ingredients:
- 7 oz (200 g) buckwheat
- 1 onion
- 1 egg
- 5 mushrooms (champignons)
- 0.7-1 oz (20-30 g) any hard cheese
- Salt and pepper to taste
- 1 tbsp ghee (clarified butter)

Instructions:
1. Pour boiling water over the buckwheat (about 0.6 inches above the buckwheat), cover it, and let it sit for 30-60 minutes until cooked.
2. Boil the egg and grate the cheese.
3. Chop the onion and sauté it in ghee until golden. Add the sliced mushrooms and sauté for another 2-3 minutes.
4. Add the chopped egg and buckwheat to the pan. Stir everything together.
5. When serving, sprinkle the dish with grated cheese.

Nutritional Information (per serving):
Calories: 350 kcal, Fats: 15g, Carbs: 40g, Protein: 15g, Fiber: 8g, Cholesterol: 0.15g, Sodium: 0.04g, Potassium: 0.5g.

Spicy Vegetarian Rice with Vegetables
(2 servings, 30 minutes, gluten-free, vegetarian)

Ingredients:
- 7 oz (200 g) long-grain brown rice (a mix of red, black, and brown rice)
- 1 medium carrot
- 1 onion
- 2 garlic cloves
- 1.8 oz (50 g) cauliflower
- 1.8 oz (50 g) broccoli (or any vegetables you prefer)
- Spices to taste (coriander, cumin, turmeric, paprika, pepper)
- Salt to taste
- 2 tsp ghee (clarified butter)
- 2 tbsp pumpkin seed oil (or olive oil)

Instructions:
1. Soak the rice in water for a couple of hours or overnight. Drain the soaking water and add fresh water in a 1:1 ratio. Bring the rice to a simmer over medium heat. **Tip**: If the water evaporates too quickly, add a little hot water.
2. Grate the carrot, mince the garlic, and finely chop the onion and cauliflower. Sauté the vegetables in ghee with a little water. After about 10 minutes, when the rice is cooked, mix the rice with the vegetables. Season with salt and serve.

Nutritional Information (per serving):
Calories: 320 kcal, Fats: 14g, Carbs: 40g, Protein: 6g, Fiber: 8g, Cholesterol: 0.05g, Sodium: 0.03g, Potassium: 0.5g.

Potato Pizza with Cheese
(4 servings, 30 minutes, gluten-free)

Ingredients:
- 3 large potatoes
- 2 eggs
- 4 tbsp any gluten-free flour (rice, etc.)
- Salt and pepper to taste
- 1 tbsp butter or ghee for greasing
- 1.8 oz (50 g) hard cheese

Instructions:
1. Grate the potatoes on a coarse grater, squeeze out the excess juice, and add 2 eggs, flour, salt, and pepper. Mix well.
2. Line a baking dish with parchment paper, grease it with butter, and spread the "potato dough" evenly.
3. Bake for about 30-40 minutes at 350°F (180°C) until a light golden crust forms.
4. Once the crust is ready, sprinkle grated cheese on top and return to the oven for another minute to allow the cheese to melt slightly.

Nutritional Information (per serving):
Calories: 280 kcal, Fats: 12g, Carbs: 32g, Protein: 10g, Fiber: 4g, Cholesterol: 0.15g, Sodium: 0.04g, Potassium: 0.7g.

Sea Bass Baked with Sweet Potatoes
(2 servings, 40 minutes, gluten-free)

Ingredients:
- 1 sea bass (or dorado/any fish you like)
- 3 slices of lemon
- Salt and pepper to taste
- Spices to taste (turmeric, coriander, paprika)
- 2 sweet potatoes (or regular potatoes)
- 1 onion
- 2 tsp ghee (clarified butter)

Instructions:
1. Clean the fish, removing the insides. Slice the lemon. Place the fish on parchment paper greased with butter. Insert 3 slices of lemon inside the fish. Rub the fish with salt and sprinkle with black pepper on both sides.
2. Peel the sweet potatoes (or regular potatoes) and cut them into round slices. Place them around the fish. Season with spices to taste.
3. Bake for about 40 minutes at 350°F (180°C). Avoid over-browning the sweet potatoes and after about 10 minutes, add a bit of water to the baking dish if needed. Then continue baking until the fish and sweet potatoes are fully cooked.

Nutritional Information (per serving):
Calories: 350 kcal, Fats: 12g, Carbs: 45g, Protein: 18g, Fiber: 6g, Cholesterol: 0.1g, Sodium: 0.04g, Potassium: 0.7g.

Scrambled Eggs with Shrimp, Quinoa, and Avocado
(2 servings, 20 minutes, gluten-free)

Ingredients:
- 500 ml water
- 7 oz (200 g) quinoa
- 10.5 oz (300 g) frozen peeled shrimp
- 2 eggs
- 1 ripe avocado
- 1 tsp ghee (clarified butter)
- 2 tbsp pumpkin seed oil (or olive oil)
- Juice of ¼ lemon
- Salt and pepper to taste

Instructions:
1. Soak the quinoa in water for an hour, then drain and refill with clean water. Cook until done and cover with a lid.
2. Boil the shrimp until cooked.
3. Crack the 2 eggs into a frying pan greased with ghee and cook until done.
4. When everything is ready, serve the eggs, mashed avocado, quinoa, and shrimp on one plate, drizzled with lemon juice.

Nutritional Information (per serving):
Calories: 450 kcal, Fats: 20g, Carbs: 35g, Protein: 28g, Fiber: 8g, Cholesterol: 0.3g, Sodium: 0.04g, Potassium: 0.7g.

Cauliflower Pizza with Cheese
(4 servings, 30 minutes, gluten-free)

Ingredients:
- 1 head of cauliflower
- 2 eggs
- Salt and pepper to taste
- 1 tsp ghee (clarified butter) for greasing
- 3 tbsp any gluten-free flour (rice, etc.)
- 0.7-1 oz (20-30 g) of any rich cheese (Parmesan, sheep's cheese, goat cheese, mozzarella)

Instructions:
1. Grate the cauliflower, then add the eggs, pepper, salt, and flour. Mix well.
2. Line a baking dish with parchment paper and grease it with ghee.
3. Spread the mixture evenly in a thin layer and bake in the oven for about 30 minutes at 350°F (180°C) until golden brown.
4. Remove the baked crust from the oven and sprinkle with grated cheese. Return to the oven for another minute to melt the cheese.

Nutritional Information (per serving):
Calories: 200 kcal, Fats: 10g, Carbs: 12g, Protein: 12g, Fiber: 5g, Cholesterol: 0.2g, Sodium: 0.04g, Potassium: 0.4g.

Pasta with Cheese and Tomato Sauce
(2 servings, 10 minutes, gluten-free)

Ingredients:
- 5.3 oz (150 g) gluten-free pasta (from brown rice, legumes, etc.) *I use pasta made from chickpea, lentil, and mung bean flour.*
- 2 tomatoes
- 4 garlic cloves
- 1 tsp ghee (clarified butter) for sautéing
- 8-10 basil leaves
- 1 oz (30 g) Parmesan cheese
- 2-3 tbsp olive oil

Instructions:
1. Boil water and cook the pasta for about 8 minutes.
2. Lightly blend the tomatoes and sauté them in ghee, adding chopped basil and garlic for about 3 minutes.
3. Serve the cooked pasta on a plate, pour the tomato sauce over it, drizzle with olive oil, and sprinkle with grated cheese.

Nutritional Information (per serving):
Calories: 400 kcal, Fats: 18g, Carbs: 50g, Protein: 14g, Fiber: 6g, Cholesterol: 0.1g, Sodium: 0.03g, Potassium: 0.4g.

ANTI-AGIN DINNERS

Greek Salad with Shrimp
(2 servings, 20 minutes, gluten-free)

Ingredients:
- 2 medium tomatoes
- 2 cucumbers
- 1 bell pepper
- 1.4-1.7 oz (40-50 g) feta cheese
- 10-12 olives
- 3 leaves of any salad greens
- Salt to taste
- A pinch of dried basil + a pinch of dried oregano + a pinch of dried rosemary
- Juice of ⅓ lemon
- 2-3 tbsp olive oil

Optional:
- Boiled shrimp or a piece of white fish

Instructions:
1. Dice the cucumbers and slice the tomatoes into circles. Slice the pepper into thin strips and tear the salad leaves by hand.
2. Separately, make the dressing by mixing the dried herbs, lemon juice, and olive oil.
3. Combine the vegetables with the dressing and toss.
4. For a heartier meal, add boiled shrimp or a piece of white fish.

Nutritional Information (per serving):
Calories: 220 kcal, Fats: 18g, Carbs: 10g, Protein: 8g, Fiber: 4g, Cholesterol: 0.06g, Sodium: 0.3g, Potassium: 0.5g.

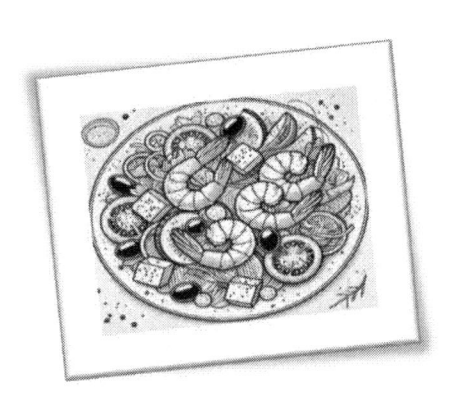

Nutritious Warm Zucchini Salad on a Green Bed
(2 servings, 20 minutes, gluten-free, vegetarian)

Ingredients:
- 1 small zucchini or summer squash
- A bunch of any greens (dill, parsley, watercress, arugula, micro greens)
- ¼ grapefruit (pomelo) or a medium tart-sweet apple
- 0.7 oz (20 g) of any clarified butter)
- 2-3 garlic cloves
- Coriander, black pepper to taste
- 2 tbsp olive oil
- Juice of ⅓ lemon

Instructions:
1. Thinly slice the zucchini into rounds. Grease a frying pan with ghee and fry the zucchini with garlic and spices until golden on both sides, for about 3-4 minutes.
2. Tear or chop the greens by hand. Slice the apple or grapefruit into thin wedges. Mix all the ingredients in a bowl and dress with olive oil and lemon juice.
3. Sprinkle with a handful of any nuts or seeds (pumpkin seeds, sunflower seeds, sesame, walnuts, pecans, or cashews work well).

- nuts, pre-soaked (about 12 pieces or a handful of any seeds)
- 1 tsp ghee (**Nutritional Information (per serving)**:

Calories: 220 kcal, Fats: 16g, Carbs: 15g, Protein: 5g, Fiber: 5g, Cholesterol: 0.03g, Sodium: 0.04g, Potassium: 0.4g.

Lentil Salad "Fantasy" with Avocado and Nuts

(2 servings, 10 minutes, gluten-free, vegetarian)

Ingredients:
- 3.5 oz (100 g) sprouted lentils (mung beans)
- 1 ripe avocado (can substitute with cucumber)
- 1 tart-sweet apple, peeled
- 0.7 oz (20 g) of any nuts (cashews, pine nuts, walnuts)
- A bunch of greens (cilantro, arugula, kale, romaine, etc.)
- Juice of ¼ lemon (optional)
- 2 tbsp olive or pumpkin seed oil for dressing
- Salt to taste

Instructions:
1. Soak the nuts in water before preparing the salad.
2. **Tip**: *Soak walnuts overnight and cashews for an hour. Pine nuts do not need to be soaked. Alternatively, pour boiling water over the nuts for 5-10 minutes before preparing the salad.*
3. Mash the avocado with a fork, chop the apple into cubes, and finely chop the greens. Combine all the ingredients with the sprouted lentils and nuts. Before serving, dress the salad with oil and lemon juice.

Nutritional Information (per serving):
Calories: 250 kcal, Fats: 18g, Carbs: 20g, Protein: 6g, Fiber: 8g, Cholesterol: 0g, Sodium: 0.04g, Potassium: 0.5g.

Buckwheat with Liver Pancakes
(2 servings, 30 minutes, gluten-free)

Ingredients:
- 7 oz (200 g) buckwheat
- 2.2 lbs (1 kg) chicken liver
- 1 carrot
- 2 garlic cloves
- 1 onion
- 1.4 oz (40 g) butter
- 1 egg
- 4 tbsp any gluten-free flour (rice, etc.)
- Salt to taste
- Black pepper to taste

Instructions:
1. Pour boiling water over the buckwheat (about 0.6 inches/1.5 cm above the buckwheat), cover it with a lid, and let it sit for 30-60 minutes to cook.
2. Grate the carrot, chop the onion, and mince the garlic. Sauté the vegetables in a pan for 3-4 minutes, adding 1 tbsp of butter. Add the chopped liver and sauté for another 8-10 minutes with the lid on. In the end, add 40 g of butter and let the mixture cool down.
3. Place the liver and vegetables into a blender and blend until smooth. Add the egg, flour, salt, and pepper, and mix well. Fry the liver pancakes in butter for about 2-3 minutes on each side.

Nutritional Information (per serving):
Calories: 500 kcal, Fats: 28g, Carbs: 32g, Protein: 25g, Fiber: 5g, Cholesterol: 0.4g, Sodium: 0.04g, Potassium: 0.6g.

Stewed Lentils with Onion and Carrots
(2 servings, 20 minutes, vegetarian, gluten-free)

Ingredients:
- 1 small onion
- 1 carrot
- 1 cup lentils
- 1.7 oz (50 g) water
- Salt, pepper, spices to taste (coriander, cumin, etc.)
- 2 tbsp ghee or butter

Instructions:
1. Soak the lentils in water overnight.
2. Chop the onion and grate the carrot. Sauté them in a pan for 3-4 minutes, adding 1 tbsp of butter or ghee.
3. Add the soaked lentils, some water, salt, and spices to taste. Cover the pan and simmer the lentils until tender, stirring occasionally.

Nutritional Information (per serving):
Calories: 240 kcal, Fats: 12g, Carbs: 25g, Protein: 8g, Fiber: 8g, Cholesterol: 0.03g, Sodium: 0.04g, Potassium: 0.5g.

Buckwheat with Mushrooms and Basil-Avocado Sauce
(2 servings, 20 minutes, vegetarian, gluten-free)

Ingredients:
- 7 oz (200 g) brown buckwheat
- 1 onion
- 1 egg
- 5 mushrooms
- 1 oz (20-30 g) hard cheese of your choice
- Salt and pepper to taste
- 1 tbsp butter (or ghee)
- ⅓ cup cashews (or pine nuts)
- 3 basil leaves
- ½ avocado
- 4 tbsp olive oil
- 2 garlic cloves (optional)
- Salt to taste

Instructions:
1. Pour boiling water over the buckwheat (about 1 inch above the level of the buckwheat), cover, and let it sit for 30-60 minutes until cooked.
2. Chop the onion and sauté it in butter until golden. Add sliced mushrooms and cook for another 2-3 minutes. Then add the cooked buckwheat and stir everything together.
3. For the sauce, blend the cashews, a pinch of salt, avocado, and basil in a blender until smooth.
4. Heat the buckwheat again in the pan with a little ghee. When serving, pour the sauce over the buckwheat and garnish with fresh greens.

Nutritional Information (per serving):
Calories: 420 kcal, Fats: 26g, Carbs: 40g, Protein: 12g, Fiber: 7g, Cholesterol: 0.1g, Sodium: 0.05g, Potassium: 0.45g.

Stewed Liver with Vegetable Salad
(4 servings, 20 minutes, gluten-free)

Ingredients:
- 1.5 lb (700 g) chicken or beef liver
- 1 carrot
- 1 onion
- 1 oz (30 g) butter or ghee
- Salt and black pepper to taste
- 2 cucumbers
- 2 tomatoes
- Bunch of any fresh greens (parsley, dill, basil, cilantro, arugula, etc.)
- 2 tbsp olive oil

Instructions:
1. Clean the liver from membranes, cut it into small pieces, and soak in cold water for one hour.
2. Grate the carrot and finely chop the onion. Sauté the vegetables in butter until they soften. Add the liver, season with salt and pepper, and simmer over medium heat for 10-15 minutes. Stir occasionally until cooked through.
3. Slice the vegetables and chop the greens. Drizzle with olive oil and serve alongside the liver.

Nutritional Information (per serving):
Calories: 320 kcal, Fats: 23g, Carbs: 12g, Protein: 22g, Fiber: 4g, Cholesterol: 0.35g, Sodium: 0.04g, Potassium: 0.45g.

Brown Rice with Shrimp and Salad
(2 servings, 30 minutes, gluten-free)

Ingredients:
- 1 1/3 cups (300 g) brown rice
- 1 carrot
- 1 onion
- 2 cloves of garlic
- Spices to taste (a pinch of cumin, coriander, turmeric)
- Black pepper and salt to taste
- 2 tbsp butter or ghee
- 10-14 oz (300-400 g) frozen shrimp (or chicken breast)
- Juice of 1/3 lemon for drizzling over shrimp (optional)
- 2 raw eggs (optional) to increase satiety

Instructions:
1. Soak the rice for 1-2 hours (or overnight). Drain and add fresh water, using 2 times as much water as rice. Bring to a boil and cook until tender.
2. Boil water and add the shrimp. Boil for 3-4 minutes until they float, then remove from heat and drain.
3. Grate the carrot, finely chop the onion, and crush the garlic. Sauté the vegetables in a pan with butter or ghee and add the spices. Then add the cooked rice and stir.
4. Pour the raw eggs into the rice with vegetables and stir. Cook, stirring, for 1-2 minutes until the eggs are cooked. Season with salt and pepper to taste.
5. Serve the rice with shrimp, drizzled with lemon juice if desired.

Nutritional Information (per serving):

Calories: 420 kcal, Fats: 15g, Carbs: 48g, Protein: 30g, Fiber: 5g, Cholesterol: 0.35g, Sodium: 0.6g, Potassium: 0.45g.

Scrambled Eggs with Shrimp and Vegetables
(2 servings, 20 minutes, gluten-free)

Ingredients:
- 3-4 eggs
- 300 g (10 oz) boiled shrimp
- 1 ripe avocado
- 1 tomato
- Any fresh greens of your choice (dill, parsley, cress, arugula, micro greens)
- 2 cloves garlic
- Coriander (optional)
- Juice of 1/4 lemon
- 1 tsp butter (or ghee)
- 2 tbsp olive oil (or pumpkin seed oil, walnut oil, etc.)

Instructions:
1. Heat a skillet with butter and sauté the shrimp with minced garlic for 1-2 minutes. Season with salt and finish with a drizzle of lemon juice.
2. In another skillet greased with oil, crack the eggs and scramble them, stirring constantly until fully cooked.
3. Combine the scrambled eggs, shrimp, avocado, tomato, and greens on a plate. Serve immediately.

Nutritional Information (per serving):
Calories: 320 kcal, Fats: 23g, Carbs: 5g, Protein: 26g, Fiber: 3g, Cholesterol: 0.38g, Sodium: 0.45g, Potassium: 0.35g.

Spicy Stewed Lentils with Chicken
(2 servings, 20 minutes, gluten-free)

Ingredients:
- 14.1 oz (400 g) sprouted lentils
- 1 onion
- 1 carrot
- 2 cloves of garlic
- Coriander, black pepper, cumin (optional)
- 14.1 oz (400 g) chicken breast
- 2 tsp butter or ghee
- 1 tbsp olive oil (or pumpkin seed oil)

Instructions:
1. Grate the carrot, mince the garlic, and finely chop the onion. Sauté the vegetables with spices in a pan greased with butter or ghee for 3-4 minutes. Then add the lentils and cover the pan. Add a little water and simmer for another 5-7 minutes.
2. Cut the chicken breast into pieces; add to another pan greased with olive oil, and cook for about 10 minutes with the lid on, stirring occasionally.
3. Combine the lentils and chicken on a plate, and drizzle with olive oil or pumpkin seed oil.

Nutritional Information (per serving):
Calories: 480 kcal, Fats: 22g, Carbs: 30g, Protein: 45g, Fiber: 10g, Cholesterol: 0.18g, Sodium: 0.15g, Potassium: 0.6g.

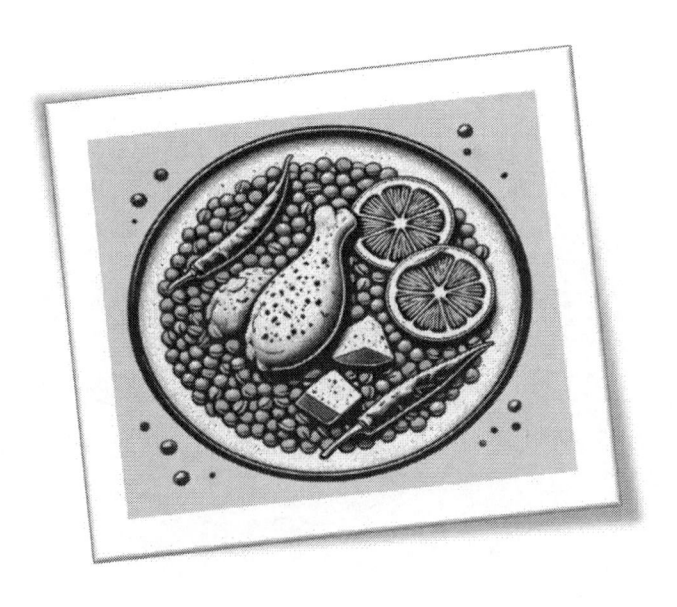

Hummus with Carrot and Cucumber Sticks
(2-3 servings, 20 minutes, gluten-free, for vegetarians)

Ingredients:
- 200 g (7 oz) dried chickpeas
- Juice of 1/3 lemon
- 4 cloves garlic
- Salt to taste
- 1 medium carrot
- 2 cucumbers
- 2 tbsp olive oil

Instructions:
1. Soak the chickpeas overnight in water. Drain and add fresh water in a 1:3 ratio (3 times more water than chickpeas) and cook until tender, about 20 minutes.
2. Blend the cooked chickpeas with lemon juice, garlic, and salt until creamy. If the consistency is too thick, add some warm water.
3. Thinly slice the carrots and cucumbers into sticks.
4. Drizzle the hummus with olive oil and serve with the carrot and cucumber sticks.

Nutritional Information (per serving):
Calories: 210 kcal, Fats: 8g, Carbs: 28g, Protein: 7g, Fiber: 8g, Cholesterol: 0g, Sodium: 0.03g, Potassium: 0.25g.

Baked Salmon with Salad
(2 servings, 30 minutes, gluten-free)

Ingredients:
- 10-14 oz (300-400 g) salmon steak (or trout)
- 2 tomatoes
- 2 cucumbers
- A handful of fresh greens (dill, parsley, arugula, micro greens, etc.)
- A pinch of rosemary
- 2 tbsp olive oil (or pumpkin seed oil, mustard oil, walnut oil, etc.)
- 1 tsp butter or ghee
- Juice of 1/4 lemon
- Black pepper and salt to taste

Instructions:
1. Grease parchment paper with butter and place the salmon steak on top. Season with salt, pepper, and a few rosemary leaves. Wrap the parchment around the steak as you would a candy. Bake at 180°C (350°F) for 20-25 minutes. *Use a fork to check if the salmon is cooked through.*
2. Slice the vegetables and drizzle with olive oil.
3. Once the fish is done, serve it on a plate with the salad, and drizzle everything with lemon juice.

Nutritional Information (per serving):
Calories: 400 kcal, Fats: 30g, Carbs: 8g, Protein: 27g, Fiber: 3g, Cholesterol: 0.08g, Sodium: 0.02g, Potassium: 0.5g.

Fried Eggs with Shrimp, Quinoa, and Avocado
(2 servings, 20 minutes, gluten-free)

Ingredients:
- 500 ml water
- 7 oz (200 g) quinoa
- 10 oz (300 g) frozen peeled shrimp
- 2 eggs
- 1 ripe avocado
- 1 tsp butter or ghee
- 2 tbsp pumpkin oil (or olive oil)
- Juice of 1/4 lemon
- Salt and pepper to taste

Instructions:
1. Soak the quinoa in water for 1 hour, then drain and add fresh water. Cook until done and cover with a lid.
2. Boil the shrimp for 3-4 minutes.
3. Heat a pan with butter and fry the eggs.
4. Serve the fried eggs with shrimp, quinoa, and mashed avocado, drizzled with lemon juice.

Nutritional Information (per serving):
Calories: 350 kcal, Fats: 20g, Carbs: 25g, Protein: 25g, Fiber: 6g, Cholesterol: 0.4g, Sodium: 0.5g, Potassium: 0.6g.

Chicken Liver Mousse with Quinoa and Carrots

(3-4 servings, 30 minutes, gluten-free)

Ingredients:
- 1.8 oz (50 g) quinoa
- 1 carrot
- A handful of arugula
- 10-12 cherry tomatoes

For the chicken liver mousse:
- 2.2 lbs (1 kg) chicken liver (or veal liver)
- 1 carrot
- 2 cloves of garlic
- 1 onion
- 0.7 oz (20 g) butter
- Salt, black pepper to taste

Instructions:
1. Grate the carrot. Finely chop the onion and press the garlic. Sauté the vegetables for 3-4 minutes in a pan with 1 tsp butter. Then, add the raw liver cut into pieces. Cover with a lid and cook for 8-10 minutes.
2. Add butter, salt, pepper, and stir. Blend the liver and vegetables in a food processor until smooth.
3. Cook the quinoa for about 5 minutes, then turn off the heat and cover with a lid.
4. Serve the mousse with sliced carrot sticks, arugula, cherry tomatoes, and quinoa.

Nutritional Information (per serving):
Calories: 390 kcal, Fats: 28g, Carbs: 16g, Protein: 28g, Fiber: 4g, Cholesterol: 0.5g, Sodium: 0.6g, Potassium: 0.7g.

ANTI-AGIN DESSERTS
Delicate Carrot Pie "Delight"
(6-8 servings, 40 minutes, gluten-free)

Ingredients:
- 17.6 oz (500 g) carrots (or pumpkin)
- 1 egg
- 1 tsp butter (ghee)
- 1 banana
- Zest of ½ lemon
- 1 tsp baking soda
- 1 tsp cinnamon
- 0.5 tsp nutmeg (optional)
- 9 tbsp gluten-free flour (whole grain or rice flour)
- 5 walnuts (optional)
- 1 handful raisins
- 1 tsp butter (ghee) for greasing the pan

Instructions:
1. Grate the carrots. Mix the flour, spices, zest, egg, and butter. Mash the banana with a fork and add it to the dough. Dissolve the baking soda with a few drops of lemon juice and hot water. Add the grated carrots, raisins, and chopped walnuts to the dough and mix thoroughly.
2. Grease a baking dish with butter. Pour the dough into the dish and bake for 30 minutes at 180°C (350°F).
3. *Tip*: *perfect for days when you have a sweet tooth* ☺

Nutritional Information (per serving):
Calories: 220 kcal, Fats: 8g, Carbs: 35g, Protein: 3g, Fiber: 4g, Cholesterol: 0.06g, Sodium: 0.18g, Potassium: 0.35g.

Homemade Chocolate
(2 servings, 20 minutes, gluten-free, vegetarian)

Ingredients:
- 3.5 oz (100 g) cacao mass
- 2.8 oz (80 g) cacao butter
- A pinch of sea salt
- 2 tbsp honey or date syrup
- 1.8 oz (50 g) of any chopped nuts

Instructions:
1. Melt the cacao butter and grated cacao in a water bath, add salt, and honey, and stir. Pour the mixture into molds and add the nuts.
2. Place in the refrigerator to set for 2 hours.

Nutritional Information (per serving):
Calories: 450 kcal, Fats: 38g, Carbs: 23g, Protein: 6g, Fiber: 7g, Cholesterol: 0g, Sodium: 0.02g, Potassium: 0.45g.

Pumpkin Chocolate Mousse
(2 servings, 60 minutes, gluten-free, vegetarian)

Ingredients:
- 7 oz (200 g) roasted pumpkin (sweet varieties)
- 2 ripe bananas (overripe is best)
- 0.5 oz (14 g) cocoa powder
- 1.4 oz (40 g) cocoa butter
- 1.7 oz (50 ml) coconut milk
- A pinch of salt
- 1/2 tsp ghee or butter

Instructions:
1. Peel the pumpkin, cut it into small pieces, and wrap it in parchment paper greased with butter. Bake in the oven for 30-40 minutes at 180°C (350°F) until soft. Once it is done, remove it from the oven and let it cool.
2. Heat the coconut milk in a pan and add the cocoa butter, allowing it to melt completely.
3. In a blender, combine the pumpkin, bananas, cocoa powder, salt, and the melted coconut milk mixture with cocoa butter. Blend until creamy, and then pour into molds. Refrigerate for 4-5 hours until set.

Nutritional Information (per serving):
Calories: 320 kcal, Fats: 22g, Carbs: 29g, Protein: 3g, Fiber: 5g, Cholesterol: 0g, Sodium: 0.04g, Potassium: 0.5g.

Carrot Cookies
(5-6 servings, 50 minutes, gluten-free)

Ingredients:
- 3 medium carrots
- 1 egg
- 2 medium bananas
- 1/2 cup (60 g) of any whole grain gluten-free flour
- 2 tbsp raisins
- 2 tbsp any nuts (I used cashews)
- 1 tsp ghee or butter

Instructions:
1. Grate the carrots, mash the bananas with a fork, add the eggs, salt, flour, and mix everything. Quench baking soda with lemon juice, mix with the dough, and add the raisins and nuts.
2. Grease parchment paper with butter and form cookies.
3. Bake at 160°C (320°F) for 20-25 minutes, then at 180°C (350°F) for another 10 minutes.

Nutritional Information (per serving):
Calories: 150 kcal, Fats: 6g, Carbs: 20g, Protein: 3g, Fiber: 3g, Cholesterol: 0.1g, Sodium: 0.02g, Potassium: 0.25g.

Baked Apples with Honey and Nuts
(4-5 servings, 50 minutes, gluten-free)

Ingredients:
- 4-5 medium apples
- 5 walnuts
- 1 tsp honey
- A pinch of cinnamon
- 1 tsp ghee or butter

Instructions:
1. Grease parchment paper with butter, line a baking dish with it, and place the apples inside.
2. Bake in the oven for 30-40 minutes at 180°C (350°F) until the apples are soft enough to be easily pierced with a fork.
3. Once done, remove the dish from the oven, sprinkle the apples with cinnamon, crushed walnuts, and drizzle with honey if desired.

Nutritional Information (per serving):
Calories: 150 kcal, Fats: 5g, Carbs: 25g, Protein: 2g, Fiber: 4g, Cholesterol: 0g, Sodium: 0.01g, Potassium: 0.2g.

Chocolate Banana Ice Cream
(2 servings, 5 minutes, gluten-free)

Ingredients:
- 2 frozen bananas (best to cut them into pieces before freezing)
- 30-40 ml of water
- 1-1.5 tbsp cocoa powder
- A pinch of salt

Instructions:
1. Blend all the ingredients in a blender until smooth and creamy.

Nutritional Information (per serving):
Calories: 150 kcal, Fats: 2g, Carbs: 37g, Protein: 2g, Fiber: 4g, Cholesterol: 0g, Sodium: 0.01g, Potassium: 0.35g.

Stewed Pumpkin with Dried Apricots and Walnuts
(2 servings, 20 minutes, gluten-free)

Ingredients:
- 14 oz (400 g) pumpkin
- 5 pieces dried apricots or raisins, soaked overnight in water
- 5 tbsp coconut milk
- 0.7-1 oz (20-30 g) walnuts, soaked overnight in water
- 1 tsp ghee or butter
- A pinch of cinnamon, salt to taste

Instructions:
1. Cut the pumpkin into small cubes. Heat a pan with ghee and add the pumpkin. Reduce the heat and simmer for 10 minutes under a closed lid, stirring occasionally.
2. After 5 minutes, add the finely chopped dried apricots, coconut milk, and sprinkle with cinnamon. If needed, add a few drops of water to keep it from sticking. Cook until the pumpkin becomes soft. Turn off the heat and serve with walnuts on top.

Nutritional Information (per serving):
Calories: 230 kcal, Fats: 14g, Carbs: 22g, Protein: 4g, Fiber: 5g, Cholesterol: 0g, Sodium: 0.02g, Potassium: 0.4g.

Chocolate Pancakes
(2 servings, 20 minutes, gluten-free)

Ingredients:
- 2 bananas
- 1 egg
- 2 tbsp cocoa powder
- A pinch of salt
- 3 tbsp gluten-free flour
- 1 tsp butter or ghee for frying
- 1 tbsp butter for serving the pancakes

Instructions:
1. Mash the bananas with a fork. Add the egg, cocoa powder, flour, and salt. Mix until smooth.
2. Heat a pan with butter and pour the batter to form small pancakes. Fry on medium heat for 3-4 minutes until bubbles appear on the surface of the pancakes, then flip and cook on the other side.
3. If cooking for a larger family, use two pans. Serve the pancakes with butter.

Nutritional Information (per serving):
Calories: 260 kcal, Fats: 12g, Carbs: 36g, Protein: 6g, Fiber: 5g, Cholesterol: 0.18g, Sodium: 0.03g, Potassium: 0.45g.

Chia Seed Pudding with Berries and Banana
(2 servings, 5 minutes, gluten-free)

Ingredients:
- 4 tbsp chia seeds
- 1-1¼ cups (250-300 ml) water
- 1 banana
- 8 tbsp coconut milk
- A handful of any berries or 3.5 oz (100 g) of fruit (I used blueberries)

Instructions:
1. Soak the chia seeds overnight in 5 oz (150 ml) of water.
2. Slice the banana. Add the coconut milk to the soaked chia seeds and mix well. Layer the chia seeds, berries, and banana. If desired, you can add any other fruits or nuts.

Nutritional Information (per serving):
Calories: 270 kcal, Fats: 17g, Carbs: 24g, Protein: 5g, Fiber: 9g, Cholesterol: 0g, Sodium: 0.01g, Potassium: 0.45g.

Buckwheat Pancakes with Honey and Butter
(2 servings, 20 minutes, gluten-free)

Ingredients:
- 8.8 oz (250 g) green buckwheat
- A pinch of salt
- 1/3 cup (80 ml) water
- 4 tbsp coconut milk
- 1.5 tbsp cocoa powder
- 1-2 tbsp honey or cane sugar
- 1/4 tsp baking soda
- 1 tsp lemon juice or apple cider vinegar
- 1 tsp ghee butter for frying

Instructions:
1. Soak the green buckwheat for about 4 hours, and then rinse it thoroughly to remove any slime. Spread it on a plate and leave in a warm place to sprout for about 24 hours, occasionally moistening it. When small sprouts appear, the buckwheat is ready to use.
2. Blend the sprouted buckwheat with water, salt, cocoa, honey, and coconut milk until smooth. Add the baking soda to the mixture and neutralize it with lemon juice or vinegar. Grease a pan with ghee and pour the batter onto it, forming pancakes. Cook for about 2-3 minutes on one side until bubbles appear, then flip and cook for another minute. Serve with honey and butter.

Nutritional Information (per serving):
Calories: 280 kcal, Fats: 12g, Carbs: 35g, Protein: 6g, Fiber: 5g, Cholesterol: 0g, Sodium: 0.01g, Potassium: 0.22g.

Nutty "Hedgehogs"
(2 servings, 5 minutes, gluten-free)

Ingredients:
- 1/2 cup (about 60 g) soaked walnuts (soak overnight)
- 1 banana
- 3-4 dates (or figs/dried apricots soaked overnight)
- A pinch of sea salt
- A pinch of cinnamon

Instructions:
1. Cut the banana and dried fruits into pieces.
2. Blend all the ingredients together, but not completely, leaving chunks of nuts and dried fruits. Shape the mixture into small balls (or use molds) and refrigerate for 3-4 hours.

Nutritional Information (per serving):
Calories: 250 kcal, Fats: 18g, Carbs: 22g, Protein: 5g, Fiber: 4g, Cholesterol: 0g, Sodium: 0.01g, Potassium: 0.3g.

Sourdough Bread with Butter and Herbal Tea
(2 servings, 5 minutes, gluten-free)

Ingredients:
- 1 slice of whole grain bread (can substitute with green buckwheat bread or **flaxseed buns**)
- 0.71 oz (20 g) butter
- Any herbal tea (Ivan tea, currant leaves, etc.)

Instructions:
1. Spread the butter on the bread and enjoy.

Nutritional Information (per serving):
Calories: 180 kcal, Fats: 12g, Carbs: 15g, Protein: 3g, Fiber: 2g, Cholesterol: 0.03g, Sodium: 0.02g, Potassium: 0.1g.

Flaxseed Buns
(6 servings, 60 minutes, gluten-free)

Ingredients:
- 7 oz (200 g) flaxseeds (ground into flour in a blender)
- 3 eggs
- 1 oz (30 g) melted butter
- 3 tbsp coconut milk or regular water
- 2 tbsp honey
- ½ tsp salt
- 2 oz (50 g) pumpkin seeds
- ¼ cup (50-70 ml) warm water
- 3 tbsp any gluten-free flour (buckwheat, rice, etc.)
- ½ tsp baking soda
- A few drops of lemon juice

Instructions:
1. Mix the flaxseed flour with eggs, melted butter, and coconut milk. Stir well with a silicone spatula.
2. Add salt, honey, pumpkin seeds, and warm water, then mix.
3. Quench the baking soda with lemon juice and add to the dough. Mix again, add 3 tbsp of gluten-free flour, and knead the dough. Shape into small balls.
4. Bake for 20-25 minutes at 175°C (350°F) until golden brown.

Nutritional Information (per serving):
Calories: 280 kcal, Fats: 22g, Carbs: 9g, Protein: 9g, Fiber: 7g, Cholesterol: 0.15g, Sodium: 0.2g, Potassium: 0.35g.

*See tips on the next page

Tips

Buns can be prepared in two ways:

1) As an addition to the first and second courses, just add 1 tbsp. of your favourite spices to the dough (ground coriander, ground cumin, dill, cilantro, etc. - to your taste).

2) Also as an addition to tea, instead of cakes, candies and other "harmful" sweets, add a handful of chopped dried prunes or apricots, raisins, cranberries, etc. to the dough to your taste.

Fruit Salad with Coconut-Nut Dressing
(2 servings, 5 minutes, gluten-free)

Ingredients:
- 7 oz (200 g) any fruits (I used mango, pomelo, and banana)
- Dressing of your choice
- 4 tbsp coconut milk
- 3-4 walnuts, soaked in water overnight (or any other nuts)

Instructions:
1. Cut the fruits into pieces, dress with coconut milk or coconut yogurt, and sprinkle with crushed walnuts.

Nutritional Information (per serving):
Calories: 220 kcal, Fats: 14g, Carbs: 21g, Protein: 3g, Fiber: 4g, Cholesterol: 0g, Sodium: 0.02g, Potassium: 0.3g.

Banana-Chocolate Cake
(2 servings, 50 minutes, gluten-free)

Ingredients:
- 14 oz (400 g) pre-soaked green buckwheat (rinsed well)
- 3 bananas (preferably overripe)
- 2 tbsp cocoa powder (heaped)
- A pinch of salt
- 2-3 tbsp honey or cane sugar
- 6 tbsp coconut milk
- A handful of raisins
- A handful of walnuts
- ½ tsp baking soda
- 1 tsp lemon juice or apple cider vinegar
- ½ tbsp ghee or butter

Instructions:
1. Combine the buckwheat, 2 bananas, cocoa, salt, and sugar in a blender. Blend until creamy. Pour the batter into a bowl.
2. Quench the baking soda with vinegar and mix with the dough; add the crushed walnuts and raisins.
3. Grease a baking pan with butter, pour the dough in, slice the remaining banana in half, and place on top. Bake at 180°C (350°F) for 45 minutes.
4. Serve with butter or ghee.

Nutritional Information (per serving):
Calories: 390 kcal, Fats: 14g, Carbs: 63g, Protein: 9g, Fiber: 8g, Cholesterol: 0g, Sodium: 0.3g, Potassium: 0.6g.

TIPS FOR SUCCESS ON THE KETO-DIET

How to Drink Water Correctly to Activate Natural Body Rejuvenation

Place this on your fridge or somewhere visible in the kitchen, and remember it takes at least 21 days to form a new habit!

In the morning, before breakfast, drink 3.5-5 oz (100-150 ml) of warm water (around 104°F/40°C).

Ideally, divide this water into 3-4 portions. If you are not used to drinking water, take a few small sips at first. Then, after 10 minutes, drink a few more sips.

If you find it difficult to drink, try taking small sips while sitting down.

10-15 minutes before each meal, drink 3.5-5 oz (100-150 ml) of warm water (around 104°F/40°C).

One hour after eating, drink 3.5-5 oz (100-150 ml) of room temperature water.

One hour before going to bed, take a few sips of room temperature water.

Smoothies, tea, juice, and coffee do not count as water.

Important: As a side effect, you may lose 6-9 lbs (3-4 kg) in just one month, without even noticing, simply by following this hydration routine!

Guide to Dairy Products

Yogurts, fermented milk drinks, and cottage cheese are made using bifidobacteria and lactobacilli.

If you do not have a dairy intolerance, include 5-7 oz (150-200 g) of dairy in your diet around 3 times a week, but always eat them separately from other foods.

***Dairy and fermented milk products should not be combined with other foods**, except for vegetables and greens.

If you discover a dairy intolerance, try using *coconut yogurt* or cheeses that are lower in lactose, such as *goat or sheep cheeses*.

If you experience bloating, eliminate fermented dairy products made with kefir cultures, yeast, or mold. These include kefir and cheeses like *Roquefort, Camembert, Brie, Gorgonzola, Feta, and goat cheese Chevre*.

For salads, use soft, mild cheeses like *Adyghe, Sulguni, Mozzarella, or fresh cheeses from goat or sheep milk, Ricotta, and Parmesan*.

***Feta and Bryndza** can be conditionally problematic due to their sharp, tangy flavor, which is often due to yeast-based fermentation.

***Consume all fermented dairy products before 4 PM**. After this time, their digestion slows down.

Food Combinations

Food Combinations to Avoid

1. **Dairy + Fruits, Dried Fruits, or Sugar** Example: Baked cottage cheese casserole with raisins or fruit and sugar.
2. **Grains + Fruits/Dried Fruits** Example: Oatmeal with fruits or dried fruits.
3. **Potatoes + Meat** Example: Chicken with potatoes.
4. **Bread + Meat + Fish** Example: A sandwich with bread, meat, and salad.
5. **Nuts + Meat** Example: Salad with chicken and walnuts.
6. **Nuts + Fish** Example: Grilled fish with a cheese salad that contains nuts.
7. **Nuts + Eggs** Example: Omelet with a salad that includes nuts.
8. **Fruits + Meat** Example: Chicken + vegetables + fruits for dessert. Fruits and dried fruits should be eaten separately from main meals.
9. **Fruits + Fish/Seafood** Example: Baked fish with rice followed by dates.
10. **Fish + Meat**
11. **Fish + Seafood**

Conditional Combinations: Suitable if You Do not Have Serious Health Issues (Autoimmune diseases, hypothyroidism, SIBO, slow bile flow, etc.)

1. **Eggs + Bread + Cheese**

2. **Eggs + Fish**

    Example: Omelet with shrimp or poached eggs with salmon.

3. **Eggs + Sweet Potatoes + Cheese**

4. **Grains + Meat**

    Example: Chicken with brown rice.

5. **Grains + Liver**

    Example: Buckwheat with liver.

6. **Grains + Seafood**

    Example: Rice with shrimp.

7. **Legumes + Chicken**

    Example: Boiled chickpeas, beans, lentils with stewed chicken.

8. **Legumes + Fish**

    Example: Boiled chickpeas, beans, lentils, hummus with fish.

9. **Sprouted Legumes + Nuts/Seeds**

Tip: *If you want to lose weight, it is better to replace grains with vegetables and greens.*

Proper Food Combinations

1. **Potatoes/Sweet Potatoes + Vegetables + Greens**
2. **Legumes + Vegetables + Greens**

    Example: Chickpeas/mung beans/lentils + vegetables + greens.

3. **Young Legumes + Fish**

    Example: Green beans, green peas + fish.

4. **Young Legumes + Meat**

    Example: Green beans, green peas + meat.

5. **Vegetables + Grains**
6. **Mushrooms + Vegetables + Greens**
7. **Vegetables + Meat**
8. **Vegetables + Fish**
9. **Nuts + Seeds + Fruits + Vegetables**
10. **Nuts + Seeds + Vegetables** *(without grains and starches)*
11. **Dairy + Vegetables + Greens**
12. **Honey + Berries + Nuts**
13. **Avocado + Vegetables**
14. **Avocado + Seeds + Nuts**
15. **Avocado + Sprouted Legumes** *(lentils, chickpeas, mung beans)*

Note: Some fruits and berries pair well with meat, fish, and cheese, like *cranberries, lingonberries, pomegranates, grapefruit, pomelo, lemon, and lime.*

10 Fake "Health Foods" Marketed as Healthy

How marketers are cashing in on your health while you might be harming it.

1. Artificial Sweeteners

Most artificial sweeteners can do more harm than good.

For example, recent research shows that consuming <u>erythritol</u> can *increase the risk of stroke, heart attack, and blood clots by 80%.* <u>Aspartame</u>, another popular sweetener, has been linked to *headaches, allergies, depression, and liver issues.*

Additionally, many focus only on the calorie content, ignoring the sweetness factor.

When the brain does not receive the expected calories from foods containing artificial sweeteners, *it may not feel satisfied*—that fullness signals that control appetite aren't activated. This *can lead to overeating.*

2. Plant-Based Milk

Read the labels on plant-based milk carefully, as many contain added artificial preservatives and stabilizers for a longer shelf life. *These products often include synthetic vitamins that may feed harmful gut bacteria, including fungi and parasites.*

3. Sports Nutrition

Amino acids, protein shakes, and bars are often consumed as a way to get essential protein for the body. However, *overconsumption of protein can increase the load on the liver and kidneys, raising the risk of heart attack, stroke, and osteoporosis.*

Many sports nutrition products contain artificial sweeteners, stabilizers, and preservatives.

4. Cereals and Granola

Cereals and granola often come with high calorie counts due to refined carbohydrates, palm oil, and trans fats, yet they offer *low nutritional value* because most vitamins are *destroyed during processing.*

Many brands add synthetic minerals and vitamins, which can *feed harmful bacteria* and *retain water in the body,* leading to bloating and even kidney issues.

5. Fat-Free Products

These are often empty calories without the healthy fats—*a real barrier to vitamin absorption.*

Essential vitamins like A, D, E, and K, crucial for smooth skin, thick hair, and strong nails, are fat-soluble and can only be properly absorbed when consumed with natural fats.

6. Juices and Smoothies

Consuming these regularly can be risky for your health. They often contain a high amount of fructose, which can *overload your liver* if consumed frequently.

Additionally, since smoothies are soft and require little chewing, *continuous consumption may lead to digestive issues and dental problems.*

7. Vitamin-Enriched Products

Today, store shelves are filled with products fortified with minerals and vitamins. Initially, it might seem that consuming them improves our health.

However, the food industry often uses *cheap synthetic ingredients*, which can do more harm than good.

Moreover, if *you have conditions like fibroids, cysts, polyps, or other neoplasms*, as well as an *imbalance in gut health*, these synthetic vitamins might *nourish the harmful elements* instead.

8. Extruded Snacks

Extruded snacks like rice cakes, corn puffs, quick-cooking cereals, etc., are made using high-temperature processing. *Such heating can create toxic substances* that pose risks to your health.

9. Fructose

Often, fructose-based products are marketed in the health food section. However, this is usually *synthetically produced fructose*, unlike the natural fructose found in whole fruits. *If you do not have diabetes, it is best to avoid these products.*

Some research suggests that *high fructose intake* may lead to *insulin resistance* and *fatty liver disease* (non-alcoholic steatohepatitis), and it might even *contribute to the development of Alzheimer's disease.*

10. Yogurts with Fruits and Sugar

Combining dairy products with sugar and fruits can cause issues, as this combination can *promote fermentation* and create an *acidic environment* in your digestive system.

An acidic environment can become a *breeding ground for fungi and parasites*.

This can lead to digestive issues (*bloating, constipation*), *deficiencies in minerals and vitamins*, since parasites may absorb nutrients from your food before your body can. As a result, *your immune system may become more susceptible to infections and viruses*.

CONCLUSION

Embarking on a journey toward a healthier lifestyle is a gift you give yourself—a gift that keeps on giving. As you have discovered throughout *Keto-Diet Cookbook for Beginners*, the keto diet is more than just a way to shed a few pounds; it's a path to a rejuvenated, more vibrant you. By combining the principles of the keto diet with nutrient-rich, youth-enhancing recipes, this book aims to guide you toward a balanced life where looking good and feeling great go hand-in-hand.

Whether you have enjoyed the anti-aging breakfasts, indulged in energizing lunches, or delighted in the guilt-free desserts, every recipe is crafted with your wellness in mind. As you incorporate these meals into your daily routine, you're not only supporting your body's natural energy and vitality, but you're also embracing a new way of living—one that celebrates simplicity, nourishment, and the joy of eating well.

Remember, achieving your health goals is not just about the recipes you follow, but the mindset you cultivate. Take your time, enjoy the process, and be patient with yourself. Real, lasting change comes from small, consistent steps, and you are already well on your way.

May this cookbook serve as your companion on the path to health and wellness. Here is to eating well, living fully, and enjoying every delicious bite along the way. Here is to *you*— **the new, vibrant, and youthful version of yourself**.

Happy cooking, and enjoy every step of your keto journey!

With health and happiness,

Tara Broock

ABOUT THE AUTHOR

Tara Broock is a passionate advocate for healthy living and vibrant aging. With over 20 years of experience in exploring and adopting ketogenic recipes, Tara has cultivated a personal lifestyle that reflects her deep commitment to well-being and nutritional health. She has consistently used the principles of the keto diet to maintain her weight, boost her energy, and feel her best—both inside and out. Her friends and family often marvel at how she continues to look and feel younger than her years.

Tara's journey began as a personal experiment to improve her health, but it soon evolved into a way of life that she loves to share with others. Thanks to the keto lifestyle, Tara has managed to maintain approximately the same weight over many years, which also means she does not have to change her wardrobe frequently—avoiding the cycle of buying new clothes after gaining or losing significant weight. This stability is just one of the many benefits of living in keto.

Each recipe in this cookbook captures Tara's love for cooking and dedication to wellness. She believes that food can be both a source of joy and a tool for transformation, and she is excited to bring you simple, youth-enhancing recipes that support a healthier, more energetic lifestyle.

With a practical and approachable style, Tara aims to make the ketogenic diet accessible to everyone. She understands beginners' challenges, and her recipes are designed to make starting—and sticking to—the keto diet an enjoyable experience. Whether you are just beginning your journey or are looking for new inspiration, Tara invites you to join her on the path to a slimmer, healthier, and more youthful you.

***

"This book is my first edition, and I sincerely hope it brings you as much pleasure as its creation brought me. Let it become your source of inspiration and faithful companion in the kitchen. I would be delighted to hear your stories and impressions after you try my recipes!"

With love,
Tara Broock

YOUR REVIEW MEANS THE WORLD TO US

We hope you enjoyed our recipes and had fun preparing them!

If so, please share your experience by leaving a review.

Your kind words and support help others discover this book, and help us create even more delicious and healthy recipes.

We are truly grateful for amazing readers like you!

We Value Your Feedback!

Printed in Great Britain
by Amazon